# Gianna

## The Love Letters of a Saint

*Translated from the original Spanish Version*
*Fr. Adolf Faroni, sdb*

*Printed and Distributed in the U.S.A. by:*

**101 Foundation, Inc.**

PO Box 151
Asbury, NJ 08802

phone: (908) 689-8792
fax: (908) 689-1957

email: 101@101foundation.com
www.101foundation.com

ISBN: 1-890137-50-2

# TABLE OF CONTENTS

*Nihil Obstat: 5/16/2000*    *Imprimatur:*
*Rev. Msgr. J.C. Abriol*    *Rev. Fr. Francis Gustilo, SDB*
*Vicar General of the*    *Provincial*
*Diocese of Manila*

# FOREWORD

Gianna's husband Peter was asked if he was aware of having been living with a saint. His answer was: "Gianna was a good Christian, a mother who loved her children tenderly, as well as me. I have never thought she was a saint because I had the idea that sanctity should be accompanied by exceptional events. Later, I have understood what holiness is. Gianna was always a convinced Christian, an exemplary spouse, a tender wife. She always considered life as a mission."

When Peter was asked to write an article on Gianna for a newspaper, he wrote with a certain reticence: "I felt uneasy at a canonical trial because I never seemed to notice extraordinary signs in her. I surrender to the convincing considerations of Msgr. Colombo when he told me that her example would certainly do good to the Church and to many mothers. They will particularly understand that the full realization of their femininity lies in being faithful spouses. Gianna's life became for many an extraordinary example of generosity for the life of many innocents, and for the sanctity of the Church."

Gianna's pious and dramatic death is not an improvised end of routine. Sanctity and heroism are not improvised nor are they the unexpected event that circumstances have produced. "As you live, so you will die." And so it was for Gianna: she worked for it, and at what a price!

*—The translator*

# A PROFOUNDLY CHRISTIAN FAMILY

The life of Gianna bloomed in the warmth of a deeply profound Christian family—the family of Albert Beretta and Maria De Micheli.

Albert and Maria married on October 12, 1908, in the parish church of St. Bartholomew in Milan. Their "yes" was a "yes" responsible to life, and to Divine Providence.

Albert was employed in the Cantoni enterprises of Milan. As a boy, he was not so fortunate. He lost his mother at the age of four and for several years boarded in a school of orphans. He longed for a family rich in affection.

Maria, however, had the joy of living in a numerous family. From an early age she wished to become a nun, yet she accepted the advice to opt for matrimony as the will of God. Her cloister was to be her home, her domestic-church was to be where she would sanctify and educate the children in the Lord.

These are the healthy roots of Gianna. God gave to that family thirteen children, five of them died at a tender age.

Somebody recalled to mind that when Maria and Albert got married, among the many gifts she was given was a basket containing 13 children and a card attached with the words "choose" written on it. And she remarked smiling, "I want them all."

Gianna was born on October 14, 1922 at Magenta, though they lived in Milan. Mother Maria, no matter the inclemency of the weather, would take her children to Holy Mass every day. She taught them to pray to Jesus before Holy Communion and after allowing them a little while alone with the Lord, she would gather them around her and make them repeat her own prayers. They were not prayers from a book, but improvised ones—simple but most beautiful.

Thus, the child Gianna learned to know and love Jesus. Gianna would indulge in prayer after Holy Communion—her head in her hands talking to the Lord as a young lover. Her incomparable guide was her mother who made her children understand that Jesus was the first, the absolute one to love, praise, and serve. The same good example was given by her father, who would rise very early in the morning to attend the first Holy Mass.

Gianna received her first Holy Communion before six years of age. On this occasion, her parents were very close to her. Her mother, who was her first educator to the faith, took upon herself Gianna's preparation for her first Holy Communion. The contents of those dialogues are only known through the life's witness of Gianna and her brothers. The day of the first Holy Communion was a day of faith for Gianna and for her whole family.

Gianna, dressed in white, welcomed Jesus in her heart on April 4, 1928 in the parochial church of Saint Grata at Bergamo. On that day, externalities gave way to the joy of having Jesus in her heart. It was a memorable day that marked the beginning of an ever-greater friendship with Jesus as Friend and Bread of Life.

Every morning regardless of inclement weather or her studies, Gianna would accompany her mother to Holy Mass to receive Holy Communion, which had become her daily, indispensable food. She was a Eucharistic soul and could not do without the Eucharist.

St. Pius X promoted the frequent Communion of youth starting from the age of reason. This Eucharistic movement was previously fostered by St. John Bosco, who had pointed out to all the example of St. Dominic Savio, who had made his first Holy Communion at the age of seven. Having come to the Oratory of Don Bosco, St. Dominic became a daily Communicant. Following the footsteps of this saint are many other youth who found their sanctification in the frequent reception of Holy Communion and among them Gianna, the new Blessed.

## YEARS AS A STUDENT

Her parents provided Gianna and her brothers with a solid formation in Faith, and also saw to it they had a profession.

Gianna started her schooling in 1928. However, she preferred the home environment to the school one. She went to the Canossian sisters and ended her primary school with good marks. In 1930, she received Confirmation. Her difficulties began in High School. In her fourth year, she failed in Italian and Latin. There was no doubt that she was intelligent, but she had to work very hard at it. She had her dark days but was able to overcome her scholastic difficulties with perseverance.

Professor Giuseppina Tononi writes of her: "She was a dear girl who, due to her simplicity and sweetness of character and to the exquisite sensibility of her artless and candid soul, knew how to draw to herself the sympathy and affection of those who approached her. She was like a flower blooming in the warm and serene intimacy of her family. She was an attentive and serious student. I never heard from her a word of annoyance, or of rebellion."

Gianna remained dedicated to her studies because she knew that diligence in this respect was the will of God. In spite of her hard work, her relations with God did not suffer. Her studies were an instrument for her professional formation but God always remained her first and foremost aim. She never sacrificed the duties of faith, prayer, and youth apostolate for her studies. Her sister Virginia writes of her: "Daily meditation in the morning, was for her a source of joy, love, and strength. In the afternoon she never missed a visit to the Blessed Sacrament. She continued saying the Rosary daily, a devotion she received from her family" Her brother Albert testifies that he never saw his sister missing her daily Communion.

During her first Spiritual Retreat in March 1938, she filled up a notebook with notes, prayers, and resolutions. Here were her written resolutions:

1. I will do all for Jesus. I will offer to God every activity and pain of mine.

2. I will not go to the cinema without first knowing if the film is good.

3. I wish to die rather than commit a mortal sin.

4. I wish to fear mortal sin as if it was a snake, and I repeat: I wish to die a thousand times rather than offend the Lord.

5. I will pray the Lord to help me not to fall into hell. Therefore I will avoid whatever is bad for my soul.

6. I will say a Hail Mary asking the Lord for a good death.

7. I will pray the Lord to make me understand his great mercy.

8. I will obey and study for the love of God.

9. I want to recite my prayers, always on my knees, in my room at the foot of my bed.

10. I want to accept anything of M.M. The way to humiliation is the shortest to way to holiness.

11. I will pray the Lord to let me go to Heaven. I will always say I have fear not to go there, thus I will pray and with the help of God, I will enter the kingdom of God.

Gianna was open to all beautiful things. She loved nature. Her soul was always in dialogue with God. She would see Him in the wonderful things of creation. She felt attracted by whatever was beautiful. She loved the mountains, climbing, and skiing. She once wrote, "When I am on high mountains, with a clear sky and white snow, how I enjoy and praise God!"

Finally, the day of her graduation from Medical School came. With her spiritual adviser, she decided her calling was to sanctify herself in marriage and become a mother.

## THE COURTSHIP

Dr. Gianna had her clinic at Mesero. Her work increased quickly and it was not easy to find a substitute for her. She was well-known and esteemed and the people always requested her.

The Molla family, who lived near her clinic, also had a high esteem for her. Their son Peter, was an engineer and vice president of SAFFA, a factory that was contributing to the wealth of the town of Mesero.

Peter was an animator of Catholic Action. On Sundays, he would teach catechism to the youth and to the men of the parish. He was a very good Christian, well known and liked by people. He was very busy and hardly knew Gianna. They first met in 1949 and Peter recalled this encounter with these words:

"I met you for the first time in my life, in September 1949, in the clinic of Dr. Ferdinand to whom I went for some indispositions. We hardly looked at one another when we exchanged greetings. My first impression of you was of a person extremely pure and serious.

"I saw you again, the following year on April 21, in the Magenta Hospital, dressed in your white uniform. You had just finished a blood transfusion to my sister Teresina, whom the Lord called to share with His angels a few days later. In that circumstance, which was very painful to me, again our eyes hardly met.

"In the summer of 1950, I met you again when you opened your clinic at Mesero and hired Nurse Luigia Garavaglia who had taken lodging in my home. From

11

the second half of 1950 to November 1954, we had only a few fleeting encounters—short interchanges of greetings and some light smiles."

Peter was witness to much of the good done by Gianna: "I was already aware in those years that you were the best of ladies on every aspect: as a student and after your graduation in medicine, in your activities in Catholic Action and in St. Vincent Conferences. I knew that, as a delegate, you were also coming to my parish of Mesero to give talks to the youth of Catholic Action. I remember that my parish priest, Fr. Giuseppe Biraghi, had the highest esteem for you. I heard no contradictory opinions about you from the persons who knew you. I only heard praises for a pure soul, an exemplary witness of faith and of Christian life. I knew how unanimous were the esteem and appreciations of everyone of your family. I also knew how your patients, young and old, thought so highly of you, especially young mothers and the aged who found comfort from your loving treatment."

"I was ever more informed of the exemplary life of Dr. Gianna. All at Mesero knew that you were so competent, that you practiced medicine with the most praise-worthy dedication for the health of the sick and at the same time, took care of their souls. It was known all over town how much good, inspired by the Gospel, you were doing for the mothers and young girls who confided to you their maternity problems."

It is known that love is born from mutual esteem and respect, and at the same time, it springs from a profound knowledge of one another. Companionship, esteem, and respect make friendship while full acceptance grows to gives birth to the most noble sentiment: LOVE. This can be affirmed of Engineer Peter and Doctor Gianna Beretta. The encounters became more frequent when Gianna hired Nurse Garavaglia who was living in the Molla's home. Peter then came to know her more and began to appreciate and esteem her even more.

After the occasion of the celebration of the First Mass of Fr. Lino da Mesero, Peter writes with joy in his diary of an unforgettable encounter with Gianna:

"I remember you, with your gentle and charming smile as you were congratulating Fr. Lino and his relatives. I still remember when you were devoutly making the Sign of the Cross before breakfast. I recall you in prayer, your friendly shaking of hands, and I recall to mind the sweet and luminous smile which accompanied it."

From these words emerges the simplicity of both of Peter and Gianna and also their profound faith. Peter was fascinated by this simple and extraordinary young lady. The next day, he wrote in his diary of the first sensations of love: "I feel the serene tranquility which tells me it was an eventful encounter. Mary Immaculate has blessed me." Engineer Molla understood his vocation on the feast of the Immaculate Conception. Gianna too, some months before, while accompanying a train of sick people to Lourdes, glimpsed what God wanted from her. Near the grotto of the apparitions, she prayed in earnest to the Blessed Virgin to intercede before the Lord to make her understand which was her vocation: to leave for the missions or to do good for sick people who were all so dear to her.

Her encounters with Peter, a young gentleman, religious and honest, especially the one on the occasion of the First Mass of Fr. Lino, were already a half answer from Heaven. In fact, Peter wrote in his diary: "Tonight can be considered a decisive one for my life and aspirations. I entrust it all to the Virgin of Good Counsel."

The meetings between Peter and Gianna became more frequent, and more intimate. They spoke of their aspirations, and of their projects. They celebrated the last day of 1954 together at the Scala (the Opera theater of Milan). After the entertainment, they went to Beretta's house. Thus Gianna's family received Peter for the first time. With them, Peter toasted the New Year.

With God's help, Gianna was opening to new horizons. The two young people had many things in common, especially faith and a clear understanding of Christian marriage. In time, they came to realize how happy they were to be together and they understood that they were made for one another.

Gianna, writing to her brother Fr. Albert, expressed the following: "As I said in my last letter, the engineer Molla, the manager of SAFFA, came, and if I should tell what I think, I would not know what to say. My spiritual director told me to try, that is, to see if this is my path and then to make a decision. Pray for me, that I may truly do what the Lord wishes from me."

Fr. Albert recalls to mind that Gianna, while waiting to know with certitude the will of God, prayed much and had others pray for the same intention. This uncertainty caused her much suffering. Her friend Enrica Parmigiani remembers that Gianna, in those days, had a reflecting countenance. At the question of whether she felt sick, she answered smiling that she was well, she only needed to know the will of God with certainty: whether to leave for Brazil to help save souls, or collaborate with God through the Sacrament of Marriage—to give birth to new creatures. Her sister Virginia also remembers those days of uncertainty and discernment of the will of God.

Things developed positively in Gianna's relationship with Peter, and in a few months, and her spiritual director, Msgr. Enrico Geriani, helped Gianna, who once more turned to him for advice, to make a decision. His answer was definitive: "To so many youth it is offered to marry and when a good youth appears, such as Peter, why not marry him? There is such a need, today, of true Christian mothers! If those who are prepared to marry do not marry, how can we have good Christian families?"

In spite of this answer, Gianna's spiritual director told her to pray even more in order to have a better knowledge of what she was going to undertake, and to help avoid regretting it later.

Through the advise of her spiritual director and her parents, and with much prayer, she understood that it was the will of God to form a holy family. She accepted to become the spouse of Engineer Peter Molla.

The official proposal from Peter came February 20, 1955. For several months, their encounters became more and more frequent and they reciprocally opened their hearts, speaking of their hopes, of their aspirations, of their certitudes. Their most tender affection was a pledge of the marvelous joy they would experience in their marriage. Peter fully shared with Gianna the ideal of a Christian marriage.

The day after receiving the letter that contained the proposal of marriage, Gianna wrote for the first time to Peter. Now, sure it was the will of God, she answered the proposal of matrimony with heartfelt sentiments. She understood that the Lord wanted her to be a true Christian mother.

She replied to his letter in a most familiar way, expressing a corner of her soul: "I wish to make you happy and to be the one you desire: good, understanding, and ready for the sacrifices life will demand from us. I have not yet told you that I am a creature always craving for affection and very sensitive. While my parents were with me, it was enough to have their affection. Then, though remaining very much united to the Lord and working for Him, I felt the desire for a mother, and I found her in that dear sister of whom I spoke to you yesterday. Now there is you, whom I already love and to whom I intend to give myself to form a truly Christian family."

Their epistolary relations from then on were continuously increasing in manifestations of respect, humility, love, hope, thanksgiving to God, projects, and great religious sentiments—a true hymn to life.

The next day, Peter answered with his heart overflowing with joy: "My dear Gianna, I have read your letter several times and I kissed it. A new life begins for me, the life of your great and desired affection and of your enlightening goodness. Let us give birth to the life of a new love. I love you, most dear Gianna. Our heavenly Mother could not give me a greater and more longed-for grace. I had so much need and so much desire for the affection of a new family. Now I have you, your affection, and your gift, and I am happy. My affection is for you and with you, I wish to form my family. I want to make you happy and understand you fully."

It is interesting to note that this communion of affection and intent is above all communion of faith. After this communion of faith springs forth the project of love and life.

These first letters could not exhaust the magnitude and depth of their thoughts and sentiments. Their correspondence always revealed the intimate joy of sincere, profound, daring, pure, and strong love.

Gianna multiplied her letters, because she felt the need to manifest her confidences, her gratitude, her growing love, and Peter wrote not less, though he was overloaded with work.

To Gianna, Peter was the man sent by God to her. With him, this is God's plan, one day with the enthusiasm of faith, they will live the great mystery, the great Sacrament of Matrimony, symbol of the love of Christ for His Church, a way that must lead to sanctity. A true love—both human and Christian—human in the perfect respect for the laws of nature; Christian because they knew that love comes from God, who is love.

For these reasons, the encounters were intensely longed for. There were times when Gianna was a bit impatient when Peter was late for their appointment. On March 11, she writes:

"Dearest Peter, words fail me to give you thanks for all the attentions and kindness that you have for me. Thank you for the beautiful roses and for the hours we spent together last night. You know, often I feel a pang of conscience for stealing your time so precious for rest after a week full of work and worries, as is yours. But on the other hand, I am so happy to enjoy your company a little. I wish time would never pass when I am with you. Peter, how I wish to be able to tell all that makes up for it. Truly the Lord loves me. You are the man I wished to meet. But I do not deny that I ask myself many times: 'Am I worthy of him?' Yes, of you, Peter, because I am so unable, though I desire, to make you happy. I am afraid not to be able to achieve it. And then, I pray the Lord: 'You who see my sentiments and my good will, put a remedy and help me to become a spouse and a mother as You wish, and I think Peter too desires it.' Is this right, Peter?"

Gianna decided to spend a few days at Sestriere (a ski resort) with her sister Zita to rest, to breath pure air, to move, and to practice skiing. But her heart felt miserable, Peter was in her mind. On March 31, after receiving his telephone call, she wished to thank him and expressed her sentiments of joy:

"Dear Peter, now I am happier because I was able to hear your voice again through the telephone. As I have told you, today snow kept falling all day long, but I have skied all the same for about four hours. To add to my joy, tonight there is a magnificent starry sky. I hope tomorrow will be a fine day. Only you are missing, Peter, and I ask for the joy to have you here on Saturday and Sunday. I will come to welcome you and with you, we spend the last hours of this vacation. I give you thanks for the beautiful outing to Switzerland last Saturday. You are too good to me and I do not deserve it. I promise to be the same to you."

From Sestriere, she expressed the joy and the sorrow of a vacation far from her beloved. It is a song of joy and love:

"Today on my return from an enjoyable time of skiing, I have found your letter. I doubt you can imagine how welcome it was! How much I love you for so sweet and affectionate expressions, from which transpire the great love you have for me.

"Thank you Peter, I too love you much, and I think our love will last forever. You have such a good character and you are so intelligent that you will understand me always and we will never disagree. I am sorry that you had so much work on Monday. I follow you always with my thoughts, and if I could help you, I would do it heartily.

"Yesterday and today the sun returned in all its glory. I rose at eight in the morning because Holy Mass is at 8:30. (What a rascal I am! while you are already at work, at eight, in your office working). Believe me, I have never enjoyed Holy Mass and

Holy Communion as much as in these days. The small church is so beautiful and inviting to recollection, it is empty. The celebrant has not even an altar boy, therefore the Lord is all for me and for you Peter, because now where I am, you are there as well.

"After breakfast, we leave with our skis and then go down the snow tracks. Often, at eleven, I go with the skiers to the instructor for some training, and no boasting, I learned to ski down very difficult slopes. But be at peace, there is no danger whatsoever because where the slopes are too difficult, the instructor makes me go down the easier ones. But it is marvelous!"

On March 25 she writes, as if continuing the preceding letter: "My happiness would be complete if you were here with me to enjoy this pure air. But the next vacation we will spend together, shall we? I really would like to offer you joy and rest because you deserve it and you need it because of so much work and worries."

When Gianna returned from the mountains and resumed her work as a doctor, Peter gave her the gift of a beautiful ring.

Moved by such attention, she gave him thanks with the outpouring of her soul:

"Dearest Peter, how can I thank you for such a beautiful ring? Dear Peter, to reward you, I give you my heart and I shall love you always as I do now. I think that on the eve of our betrothal, it pleases you to hear and know that you are the dearest person to whom my thoughts, affections, and desires are continuously turned. I am waiting for nothing else but the moment that I will be yours forever. Dearest Peter, you know that it is my desire to see you and to know that you are happy. Tell me how I should be, and what I have to do to make myself such. I trust so much in the Lord and I am sure that He will help me to be your worthy spouse.

"I like to meditate often on the Epistle of the Mass of St. Anne's: 'Who will find the strong woman? The husband's heart can trust her. She will do only good, nor ever hurt him.' Peter, could I be the strong woman!? But I am so weak! I will learn to be it in your strong arms. I feel so secure near you! I ask you a favor, since today, Peter, if you notice something wrong in me, tell me, correct me, do you understand?"

The contents, the style, the religious Christian inspiration of these letters and of others reveal the soul of Gianna. She is a strong woman who does not hesitate when she knows that her betrothal, her marriage is the will of God. The first should prepare the second. It is right therefore to make oneself known as one is and know also the most hidden recesses of the soul of the partner initiating a sincere dialogue that will continue for the rest of life. Love, which is giving oneself, thus grows and becomes adult.

"Love should not have pretence. Love one another with fraternal affection. Compete in mutual estimation. Be happy in hope, strong in tribulations, fervent in prayer, ready to help those in need..." It is the life program that St. Paul proposes to the first Christians of Rome.

## THE OFFICIAL BETROTHAL

On April 11, the official betrothal took place in the church with Holy Mass and Holy Communion. The two families Molla and Beretta were there. Gianna exchanged the gift of the ring with a golden watch. Peter touched the apex of his happiness.

A few days afterwards he wrote to Gianna: "My dearest Gianna, I am still living the joy you gave me during our betrothal, the greatest joy which I wish to be yours as well, dear object of my thoughts, of all my affection and of my desires. The gift of your heart and love have found my heart all and always for you, 0 dearest Gianna!

"You are my jewel, gentle and most sweet, dear in virtue and in goodness, in beauty and smiles. I wish my love for you to be more intense than the reflection of light of the ring of our betrothal. The wonderful watch you gave me is with me in the most beautiful time of my life; the time of our love and our family. You are the strong woman that I asked for from Heaven and the heavenly Mother has given to me. I will always confide all my heart and all the love I have for you. Love me always as you love me now, be affectionate and good to me, be kind and sweet and understanding always as you are now. This is what you are doing and how I invite you to make me happy. You are the strong woman of the Bible to me. Near you my joy is perfect. I am certain you will not give me any occasion to correct you.

"To your request, I answer with the same request to you on my regard. I see you were most devout at the Mass of our betrothal, and I feel certain of the Divine blessing you warmly invoked through our dear Father Joseph."

The confidences were always at this level of joy, trust, and also of apprehension—apprehension that gradually, totally disappears.

Love, in Gianna, becomes bold, "Peter, I give you thanks for the love you harbor for me. I wished for an affectionate good man, and God has put him at my side. How I wish too to be always joy and comfort to you, while at times the fear comes to me to be a burden to you. You are tired and weary and I entertain myself with you for hours, how inconsiderate I am!"

Where can we find a dialogue so full of love, chaste, religious, vibrant, and in perfect harmony? We should be grateful to the Molla family for having preserved this interchange of affectionate letters, rich in Christian wisdom. It is written that God does not inspire profound sentiments to be lost, but that they be saved and transmitted to others. Writings reach far in time—

they can carry words of light, of consolation, of rest, a decisive word to persons whom we shall never meet, who are not yet born. To hand down to posterity what deserves to be saved is another work of charity and love. The correspondence between Gianna and Peter, if known and meditated upon, will certainly do good to many youth who intend to found a family on Christian basis.

After the official betrothal, a concern clouded their perfect joy. Gianna felt it was her duty to tell Peter about it, thus keeping the promise to tell him everything.

"My dearest Peter, I know that you feel great love for me, and having confirmed it in your letters, it fills my heart with great joy. Dear Peter think what a great grace God has bestowed on us, we should be grateful to him for this.

"Peter, I have promised you that I would tell you whatever worries me. Excuse me if now I express a doubt which makes me suffer much. I have the fear of not being welcome by your parents, not to be what they desired I should be for you. I know you have always been, and you still are the center of their affection, and now

I feel like taking you away from them, although I love them because they are your dear parents, but I do not feel for them the affection they deserve for the goodness and kindness they show to me. If I have displeased you, forgive me."

Peter did not leave her in doubt but, at once, he took pains to reassure her, clarifying things, which gave her peace:

"My dearest Gianna, your doubts and fears are unfounded. My mother, father and sisters are of the opinion that I could not have found a better woman than you to correspond to their and my expectations, to my character, and to my life. Mother, father, and sisters greatly wished and desired our encounter and union long before December and they rejoice at our affection, our betrothal, and our fast approaching date of marriage. You are the woman that my dear ones desired for me. That I am in the center of their affection, I agree, but it is equally true that for years they advised me to create my own family and for this good, they will be able to resign themselves to the fact that I am no longer all for them. They will be greatly rewarded by the joy of knowing that I am happy with my sweet companion and of the family I am about to form. Mother and father are very simple people, best of people, still at home with the old ways. How I wish you knew the treasures of heart and spirit and of sacrifice that are in mother and father!

"Is it asking too much if I desire that you be the daughter most dear to father and mother, and to my sisters their dearest sister? You are welcome and desired by me and by my dear parents. You are my beloved Gianna, whom I would like to have here beside me to hold you fast against my heart and repeat once more all my affection for you."

Every cloud disappeared forever. She joyfully answered: "After your convincing words, I am at peace and I rejoice in thinking that you are happy."

Then she gives thanks for the clinic Peter is putting up for her. She ends her short letter, which she jokingly called 'scribbles:' "I love you Peter, and you are always present to me, beginning in the morning at Holy Mass. At the Offertory, I offer my work and yours, your joys, your sufferings and then during the whole day, till night."

The days, the weeks, and months went by and both, not being any longer very young, she in her 30th year and he in his 40th year, in common agreement, they fixed the day of their marriage: September 24, 1955.

## LOVE NEEDS A HOME

In July, they began to choose the furniture for their new home. This fact offered Gianna the occasion to manifest once more her plan for conjugal life, which Peter shared wholeheartedly:

"On Sunday, while I was choosing the furniture, I was enjoying beforehand an all beautiful home, all light and new. Many thanks for your exquisite understanding and solicitude to wish to satisfy my desires. Peter, think of our nest, warmed by our affection and made joyful by beautiful "puppies" that the Lord will send us. It is true there will also be pains, but if we always love each other as we do now, with the help of God, we will be able to bear them. Now however, let us enjoy the happiness of loving one another because I have always been taught that the secret of happiness is to live moment by moment, and to give thanks to God for everything He, in his goodness, gives us day after day. Therefore, let us be optimistic and let us live happily!"

In the two and a half months before their marriage, Gianna continued to exercise her medical profession, her commitment to the girls of Catholic Action of Magenta, and the work of St. Vincent de Paul. She was ever more serene because she understood that to marry Peter was her vocation. "From following our vocation depends our earthly and eternal happiness. Every vocation is vocation to the material, spiritual, and moral maternity. God has put in us the instinct of life. The priest is the father, and sisters are the mothers of souls. Woe to those girls who do not accept the vocation to maternity, everyone should prepare to be giver of life..."

## A TRIDUUM IN PREPARATION

During the time their wedding date, Peter was loaded with work. For this reason, he absented himself for a week. He had to travel on business to Sweden, and Denmark. Gianna on the departure day writes to him: "Dearest Peter. I was worried thinking that something had happened to you, but your call brought me reassurance. My dear Peter, you know what a joy it is for me to see you and to be able to enjoy your company and, when just reasons do not allow it, the heart complains.

"Dear Peter, I wish you to feel me very near to you in these days of absence, because you cannot imagine what I feel to know that you are traveling and so far away. You might say I am exaggerating, but it is really so. You are my Peter, I already feel I am only one soul and heart with you. When I think on our reciprocal love, I give thanks to God. It is really true that love is the most beautiful sentiment that God has placed in the hearts of men. And we shall love one another always as at present, dear Peter.

Just twenty days and then, I will be Gianna Molla!"

"What do you think if, to prepare ourselves spiritually to receive this Sacrament, we have a triduum on the 21st, 22nd, and 23rd? Mass and Holy Communion, you in your place and I in the Shrine of the Assumption. Mary will join our prayers and desires, and since our union is pure, Jesus cannot but listen to us. I am sure you will say yes, and I give you thanks.

"If it pleases you, think that on the next trip, I will be really near you and I will tell you verbally, till tiring you to death, that you are all my life. A thousand thanks, Peter, for the magnificent house that you have prepared for me. More beautiful could neither be nor desired. Now it depends on me to make it ever more sweet and welcoming. Have a good trip, dearest Peter, and don't miss the train next Sunday.

Peter sent her an answer from the boat on his way to Denmark describing the panorama, the meadows, the woods and the small houses in a row. In every house he sees the one he has prepared with much love:

"At the prow of the boat which so silently moves forward on a sea of peace, I am reciting the Rosary and I am asking for every grace for you and our family from the Madonna of Good Council to the Assumption of your fervent daily prayers."

From Sodermann, a small town in Sweden, he wrote: "My first thought was for you, a thanksgiving to the Lord for having a peaceful night, and a great desire to see you again as soon as possible." And then: "Gianna, on Sunday I will see you again after an absence which seems to me so long. I wish to press you to my heart and kiss you and reassure you once more of my love."

Leaving Stockholm on the way back to Italy, he tells her he has prayed to Jesus and Mary so that: "they may bless us always, and especially in this month."

The two last writings of Peter to Gianna and of Gianna to Peter, before marriage, were still and always the manifestation of the growing love and the reproposal of a life and of a family according to the plan of God.

Peter writes to Gianna, dreaming and renewing his good resolutions and sentiments: "I have already written to you, Gianna, that the small houses of Sweden, with flowers in all windows radiating the intimate warmth of the domestic hearth, would always remind me of our small home and with the sweetness of affections with which you will enhance it.

"In the children of Sweden, who also call mother as we do 'mamma,' I foresee the gifts from heaven, your jewels, 0 Gianna, the children that God will give us for our joy and blessing.

"Just another Saturday and you will be my spouse. Gianna, I want to be the husband you dreamed of in your most joyous and holy desires; the husband worthy of your virtues, of your goodness and of your immense affection. In these days, as I never did before and above all during the triduum. I will pray to Jesus and the Heavenly Mother, and to my sister whom I feel is in Heaven, that they may bless my thoughts and be generous in graces for our new family.

"Gianna, with the certitude that God wants us united, you and I have initiated our new life. The preceding months were a continuous showing of understanding and of affection. Now our understanding is perfect, because the Divine Law is for us heavenly light and guide, because Heaven and Divine Law find in you the most beautiful virtues and the greatest goodness, and in me the deepest desire and the immense joy to make you always happy.

"Now our affection is full because we are one heart and one soul, one sentiment and one affection, because our love is able to wait, strong and pure for the heavenly blessing."

Gianna was at the peak of happiness. Once more she gives thanks to Peter for his affectionate expressions:

"Peter, how much I have to learn from you! You are of good example to me, and I give you thanks. Thus with the help of God, we will do our best so that our small family may be a cenacle where Jesus reigns over all our affections, desires and actions.

"Dear Peter, we are a few days away from marriage and I am so moved when I approach the altar to receive Holy Communion, the Sacrament of Love.

"We shall become collaborator of God in creation, thus we can give him children to love and serve him.

"Peter, will I be to you the spouse and the mother that you have always desired? I really wish it, because you deserve it and because I love you so much."

From the correspondence between Gianna and Peter, we have taken some passages. To read it entirely is not boring but edifying and moving. It reveals a marital love which enlightens at the light of Divine love. Everything is pure, human, and sacred at the same time.

# MARRIAGE

Finally September 24 arrived. It was a splendid, sunny day. Gianna, dressed in white, and accompanied by her brother Ferdinand, made her entrance in the majestic Basilica of St. Martin of Magenta.

As Gianna appeared, a clamorous applause filled the aisles. Gianna reached the altar, looking here and there with her big black eyes, in wonder for the sudden unexpected clapping of hands. It certainly was the best wishes and the thanks of the many friends and of many who had been medically helped.

The ceremony was presided over by her brother, Fr. Joseph. He too was very much moved. At the homily, he exhorted the couple, inviting them to sanctity and to living their matrimony in its Christian fullness. It was a memorable day which will live in the hearts of the young couple.

Peter will write in his memoirs, "How often the thought of the unexpected clapping of hands at your entrance in the basilica and walking to the altar comes to my mind. Your brother Joseph, who blessed it, exhorted us to give testimony to the Gospel and to sanctity."

With so many good wishes, blessed by God, and helped by the prayers of so many well-wishers, the conjugal union of Peter and Gianna set profound roots to grow exuberant, as an example to many families.

After the Holy Mass, there followed a reception in the Beretta's house. Then the spouses left by train for South Italy. They stopped in Rome where they had an audience with the Pope at Castel Gandolfo, to Pompei to pray at the shrine of the Virgin of the Rosary, then to Capri, Sicily Palermo, Syracuse, Catania, and Taormina. The honeymoon was very beautiful. They returned by plane.

After their honeymoon, Peter had important business to deal with in Germany and Holland. Accompanying him, the honeymoon continued for Gianna. Both left by train for Dusseldorf, Colonia. It was a new experience for Gianna to share in the work of her husband, to know and share his responsibilities.

Finally they were back from the long trip. Now began a life which had no routine. Every day was new and beautiful. Every day has a history of work and prayer, of worries, hopes, and love. The house Peter had prepared was a beautiful villa surrounded by trees and flowers of which Gianna took care.

Gianna resumed her work in the clinic with enthusiasm. After a time, she became director of the Home of Children and of ONMI.

Gianna was a true mother. An educator of the maternal school recalls to mind: "Gianna used to come here for the periodical medical check up of the children. She was always ready for any call and knew how to attend medically to every child with the kindness and refinement of one who really sees in them the image of God. She would bend over each one of them with delicate interest. When it was the birthday of a child, she would offer ice cream to all of them and would sit in the midst of them, just like a mother."

At Ponte Nuovo, if she was called during the night, Peter would accompany her to the sick people unmindful of her exhaustion. Since her marriage, her responsibilities have increased. Now Dr. Gianna also takes care of every corner of the house. Not withstanding her great amount of work, the day always begins with Holy Mass. She never would miss her visit to the Blessed Sacrament.

Due to the amount of work she had will her activities with her patients, she soon had to take in a maid, who she treated as a part of her family.

There was only one cloud overshadowing her daily life—the joy of a child delayed. Writing to her sister Virginia she opens up:

"Unfortunately, I do not feel the symptoms of pregnancy. Pray that the Lord sends me many children soon, good and healthy." It was her vocation to be a mother made happy by a crown of children.

How sad is the world when there are no cradles, no pregnancies. The world becomes less good when innocent souls are missing. Egoism predominates, and miserably fades the picture of mother, and the paternal one disappears. This is the social and parental contention today, the families seem to fear to have children. The generations who preceded us did not think this way, they were more humane and inclined to solidarity.

Finally the desires and prayers of the Mollas are answered. Pierluigi is born on

November 19, 1956. The house of the spouses Molla is happy, now they are a true family. Fr. Joseph, Gianna's brother who blessed the matrimony, baptized the baby a few days later. The child, as was done for children, was placed under the protection of the Virgin Mary, Mother of Good Counsel.

Gianna's professional work starts again. The house of the little children enjoys her. The children knew her as the mother of Pierluigi. They willingly go to her because she is always serene and smiling.

She attends their mothers as well, with great love and competence. She wants them to be true Christian mothers, as she was trying to be. The good mothers understand and esteem her. And they loved her because, more than a doctor, she was a true sister to them.

Her professional activities did not make her forget her brother and sisters. She loved to be with them. She reminded her brother Fr. Albert of this. On Easter day she invited all of them to her home, "Only you were missing. We were all together, here in my home, at dinner time.

"It is so beautiful to come together

from time to time! We are already tasting the joy, when, back to Italy, we will have you here with us for a few days. Think how beautiful after ten long years!"

With Peter and children, every now and then they would visit the old house at Magenta. And when Peter was absent for several days due to work, she would return to her old home and stay there several days. Affectionate and delicate with Peter's mother, she would never call her mother-in-law but "mamma."

While she was on vacation with the first born child Pierluigi, she wrote to Peter: "Give thanks to mother for her kind greetings and give my best wishes to her for me and for Pierluigi." She was always polite and affectionate with all her relatives. With the brothers, religious working far away in other lands, she never interrupted her epistolary communication showing interest for their health and above all with her sister Virginia, a missionary in India.

In one of the many letters she wrote: "I heard that you suffer much because of the hot weather. How I wish I could send you a bit of cold! Here it is raining already for three days. If you really cannot stand the weather, do not wait until you are sick, come back here; do you understand? I wonder how you are loved by all the sick people you attend. Be jolly as usual. We think on you day after day and we are near you with our prayers, I would like to do something for you, but Heaven, sea, and land separate us. May father and mother from Heaven help you to stand the weather and grant you good health. Tell me the truth about how you are, if your feet are swollen, if you need anything."

She had the same affection and interest for her brother Fr. Albert, missionary in Brazil. In a certain way, he was her spiritual director. She followed him in his spiritual work with her mind and heart. "We will be so happy to be useful to you in anything you need. We are near you always with our thoughts and prayers."

In another letter, she asked him: "How are you? You say nothing about your health in your last letter. Beware of the lepers. If you need disinfectants, write to me, I will send them to you. Try not to get too tired. Also, God rested on the seventh day..." To him and to her sister she always sent money and medicines.

# SHE WAS ABOVE ALL A SPOUSE

Gianna's main effort was to please her husband. It was a task freely and consciously done. She wanted to be the "perfect woman" of the Bible. She wrote it to him with a chaste and humble fear not to be so. "I always love to meditate the passage of the Epistle of the Mass of St. Anna: Who will find the perfect woman (strong)?" Peter, how I wish to be for you always the perfect woman, but I am so weak!"

The Bible gives a stupendous praise to the perfect ideal woman, and Gianna wanted to be similar to her and live this ideal because: "She brings him (husband) happiness all the days of her life. She is clothed with strength and dignity. She uses her mouth with wisdom, and in her tongue is kindly counsel."

The sacred text continues with expressions which seem to anticipate the future experience of Gianna: "Her children rise up and praise her. Her husband too, extols her. Many are the women of proven worth, but you have excelled them all."

Lauretta Molla, her daughter, expressed in a beautiful essay written in the classroom:

"What has remained better impressed in my mind is her image as a mother: true mother, conscious of her duties toward the family, desirous to give a moral formation and the best education to her children. In fact, even though her work kept her extremely busy, she made her best to stay with her children, who being at the early years of their lives, had the absolute need of the presence of mother to guide and follow them.

She performed the duties of a doctor with so much care and happiness. Above all she enjoyed attending the children, especially those most in need. I believe that also in the clinic she continued the work of a mother. Among a thousand thoughts she does not praise only her children but also all other children who surrounded her, in need of her assistance.

Among all the impressions I experienced, the one that is still now the most relevant in my life is the profound admiration which awakens in me the thought of a mother that gives her life for her creature. In fact, she chose to give up a joyful existence so that the creature she bore in her womb could also live and praise the Lord.

"She certainly had a great courage and I believe that few mothers would have acted thus. However I am sure that her example, of which many are acquainted, will serve to comfort all those mothers who found themselves in the same predicament. I can affirm to be really proud to have had a mother of so great courage, who was able to live as God wanted, who has served humanity with her example and work.

"I feel she is always near me in this period of my formation, and that she helps me as if she were alive."

When we think of the testimonies of those who have the fortune to know and esteem her, we have to agree that Gianna's desire to be similar to the perfect woman of the Bible was fully realized. Her husband, children, friends and today the whole Church, meditating on her life and proclaiming her virtues make a splendid praise to her, well deserved indeed!

"Many are the women of proven worth, but you have excelled them all."

The few years of conjugal life lived together in perfect harmony of faith and works, of trials and hopes and above all, of love, are the concrete realization of what the Church, in fidelity to the Word of God, teaches and instills: "The worldly family, as well, can be religious in the true sense of the Christian tradition according to the spirit of the Gospel.

Two years after her heroic death, Vatican II, in the dogmatic Constitution *Lumen Gentium* asserts, "Married partners have their own proper vocation: they must be witnesses of faith and love of Christ to one another and to their children." (35.) Gianna and Peter never forgot this thought of the Church codified in Vatican II. They were the first educators in faith and witness to their children. In *Lumen Gentium* the Christian family is described as the small domestic church, "In what might be regarded as the Domestic Church, the parents, by word and example, are the first heralds of faith in regard to their children. They must foster the vocation which is proper to each child, and this with special care if it be to religious life" (L.G. n.11).

The Christian family, as domestic church, is an ancient doctrine in the Church. Perhaps it dates back to St. Chrysostom, who used to tell his faithful: "When yesterday I said: make of your family a church, you burst out in joyful acclamations and manifested in an eloquent manner how much joy pervaded your soul on hearing those words" (Greek Patrology 54, 607f).

Peter and Gianna, as leaders of Catholic Action, knew this doctrine well. Gianna in her curriculum of Leader of Catholic Action and as simple student faced the family problems with Fr. Rotondi S.J., and other priests to whom she had listened in spiritual retreats and conferences. The Christian education, the serene witnessing of the parents and above all the familiarity with the Word of God and her sincere sacramental piety prepared her well for the duties and responsibilities as a spouse and Christian mother.

Her conjugal life, therefore, evolves with much ease. Engineer Peter Molla would find very normal what he saw in Gianna's performance. It was this daily coherence which made Gianna an exemplary mother and a perfect spouse.

## AFFECTIONATE SPOUSE AND INCOMPARABLE MOTHER

The birth of Pierluigi was a memorable event. The 1957 summer vacation in the Alps was a stupendous experience. Together with Peter, with Pierluigi on his shoulders, and away on long hiking! Gianna felt marvelously realized in her role of mother. Shortly after they announced a new conception, in December comes to light Maria Zita, usually called Mariolina. The newly arrived was baptized a few days later by Fr. Joseph. It is great joy for Gianna to press her new baby to her chest after baptism which mysteriously made the child a daughter of God, God's angel on earth.

Her professional duties press her, but Gianna does not renounce the joy of spending the greatest time possible with the two "puppies" and caring for them. Her children and her husband were her treasures and to be away from these treasures was a true suffering she bore interiorly. This would happen when Peter, had to absent himself and go abroad for some days on business. Like the Spouse of the Canticles, Gianna would wait for his return because "the great expanse of waters cannot extinguish love."

She was also worried: "Peter always had so much work and so many worries. In March, he had to go to the USA on business with several factories. "I pray that the Lord assists him! There are so many plane accidents. I am worried, but I trust in the Blessed Mother and in the prayers of the souls of purgatory." To make her happy, Peter travels long hours by train. "Be patient, golden Peter, but I am made this way! I feel more at peace." "Golden Pedrin," and "Beautiful Pedrin" were endearing names she gave to her husband.

The joyous and loving gestures of esteem were reciprocal. On the second anniversary of their marriage, Peter sends her a bouquet of flowers. Gianna at once wrote to him: "Your magnificent flowers and your most affectionate expressions have moved me so much. No end of thanks to you and to my Gigetto (Pierluigi) and above all to the Lord who loves us so much. Kisses to Gigetto and to his father. Your most affectionate Gianna."

Pierluigi also shared in the joys and anxieties of mother for the increasing trips of his father. In a letter written after the long trips to USA an d Canada, Gianna expresses her motherly anxieties. "I have received your letter on Monday this morning, always written in "Heaven" as our Gigetto says. We heard on the radio about a storm of wind and rain, and until we received the announcement from TWA that the plane had safely landed in Boston, we were all in great anxiety. My Peter, my thought is always with you. I think of you with much, much affection day and night, because I love you so much, you know it. One would wish to be ever near and united, but, let us offer it to the Lord that He may assist and help our dear, beautiful family."

Sometimes there was no communication with her husband. On one occasion the radio announced bad weather due to cold air and storm from the Atlantic. On that day, she wrote to her husband, "I wonder what a difficult trip you had! I can only pray for you and entrust you to Divine Providence." Many are the letters which show love, anxiety, hope, tenderness, and trust in God.

During her third pregnancy, she wrote to Peter who was away again on business, "I will hide from you that upon hearing the news that you cannot return until June 10, I had a knot in the throat. I cried. Then I offered the sacrifice to God for you, that he may protect you in your continuous trips and for our "pippo" whom we are expecting, that it may be born beautiful, healthy and without any defect. Thus I am in good spirits again. I have kissed many times Gigetto and Mariolina, I have pressed them to my heart and I felt you with them, very near to me as if you were already back with us."

Once more, Gianna seems to be the Spouse of the Song of Songs:

"I was sleeping,

but my heart kept vigil;

I heard my lover knocking."

On May 13, 1959, the letter she wrote to Peter, who was on a journey, is still more dense in faith: "My Peter; you can imagine how my thoughts are always with you, with your trips. Every time Gigetto prays, he says: "Jesus, provide for my father a good trip. Father come back soon. Is father falling down? No!" But separation is always painful. Last night Fr. Mariano speaking on the TV was saying that true love does not last a day, but forever. And the spouses who have constantly loved one another, upon reaching paradise, will become aware that the time during which they loved one another, was very short and will rejoice at the thought that they have the whole eternity before them to continue expressing their love. Golden Petrin, you know how much I love you, you are in my thoughts and I wish to make you happy."

The letters written to Peter when he was traveling far away on business are very much the same—full of love and tenderness—almost a passionate refrain. We can therefore imagine the affectionate level of their living together.

After some months, Laura is born and Gianna announces her unrestrained joy to a friend: "Wednesday, at 8:30 in the morning, Lauretta was borne. You can't imagine my joy, first of all because thanks to God everything proceeded well, then because she is so beautiful, good, and healthy and last, because she is a girl, and I truly desire a little sister for Mariolina. I know, by personal experience how precious are sisters, and thus the Lord heard my prayer.

Maternity for Gianna was always a suffering and painful experience. Two pregnancies had failed causing great sadness for both her and Peter. After the birth of Lauretta, she wrote: "I have continued undoubtedly my pregnancy till the end and with my usual ten days of delay. Now I am with my good Lauretta. Tonight I hope to see my two treasures who have been fifteen days at Courmayeur. They call daily and they are very happy to come and to see "the new sister." Pierluigi called last night asking to talk to her: "I wish to speak with my little sister." On his way back to Italy from America, Peter made this comment: "Gianna could not give me a better gift."

Such a family looks like a fairy tale today. But it is not so. It is the sincere and desired result of sincere souls who love to draw from the spring of Love. God is infinite love. For this reason, love prevails over every difficulty.

"For stern as death is love,

A flame of God,

Deep waters cannot quench love,

Nor floods sweep it away."

Peter's love for Gianna and Gianna's for Peter grow everyday by means of this daily religious dialogue.

In spite of all his duties, Peter does his best not to neglect his responsibilities of father and tries to balance as much as possible his duties towards the family and toward civil society. Rather, he keeps the family in first place. On July 31, Peter recalls: "We have climbed to Courmayeur, up to the new house, a villa on the meadows which I had rented from Verrand, a wonderful place, at that time still quite isolated from the town, but full of construction. Pierluigi and Mariolina were already on the mountains for quite a time, so Gianna was able to reach her "puppies" taking with her the new born baby. Together we have spent unforgettable days. I was able to stay there with my family for the whole month of August and Gianna returned to Ponte Nuovo, with the children, only at the end of September. We were very comfortable. The mountain air seemed to be just for them. Gianna would feed Laura and would take care of the two older children with all her affection, on the alert of dealing with the jealousy of Pierluigi.

"Mariolina was so happy to have a sister as to have no problems at all. For her, Laura was a true doll with whom to play, with a certain apprehension that she might not break it. Together they had long walks just in front of Mount Blanc. When I was not at home, Gianna would get the children in her car and, with Savina and Aunt Zita, would drive them to a river to have merienda. On such occasions, Pierluigi had his joy throwing stones into the waters and Mariolina, who imitated him in everything, would do the same. Ours was a peaceful life. In September, I went back to the factory, but every weekend I would visit my dear ones, and for us it was a great feast. At Mesero, the clinic was again returned to Ferdinand which gave a respite to Gianna, who, could not forget her patients.

The growing family demanded a more attentive presence of the parents. Peter and Gianna knew it, and in their heart there was already a decision. Gianna, with her preventive love, makes this question to Peter, "When we have given a brother to Pierluigi, I will give up practicing medicine, though I love it, and I will do the mother's work. They had to hurry up because Gianna was already thirty seven of age, she was no longer young. However, the fourth pregnancy proved to be tragic.

The desire for another child was the desire of both. Gianna was expecting a boy, "Fr. Enrico," a son priest to give the name of her brother who became a Capuchin and who had taken the name of Fr. Albert.

When she married she wanted a nuptial dress of white satin to use one day to make a white chasuble for a priest son. Extraordinary mother, she was! She knew that the children are a gift of God, and to give a son to God seemed to her so natural. Perhaps she heard during her years of Catholic Action Don Bosco's affirmation: "The greatest gift God can give to a family is a son priest," or she knew the other of Pius XII: "God will make the parents understand how beautiful it is to give him a son priest."° I wonder how often Gianna meditated on that very poetic verse:

"Your spouse is like a fertile vineyard, In the intimacy of her home;
   your children as olive shoots,
   around your table...
   Thus will be blessed the man
   who fears the Lord."

Gianna prayed much for this and Peter was in full agreement with her. "Both, she and I came from families with many children, and my spouse has always desired to have at least four children. How she longed to see them growing together, good and clever!" And as Gianna was close to thirty nine of age, jokingly she used to say: "We are old, and we have to hurry up."

On December 10, 1960, Peter had to go abroad. He wanted Gianna to accompany him. The children were left to her sister Zita and to the maid Savina and they left for England and Holland. They were most beautiful days with a new experience for Gianna, who, however, did not let a day pass without telephone calls to ask about her children and to hear their voices. She returned on the 18th. Christmas is near and she prepares the crib with her children. She rejoices in working with them.

In January 1961, Gianna felt the need for a period of rest and went to the mountains. On her return, she is with Peter, who is busy with meetings and discussions with the labor unions. At SAFFA, the factory, people live hard days on strike. Peter had to control himself and not lose his temper, he had to hear the workers' whistle and not mind it. Gianna, with her affectionate patience, encourages him. When the strike is over, Gianna writes to Virginia: "At present, the workers are peaceful and working, let us hope for the better. On

Wednesday, Peter is in Germany and the following week he will leave for Paris and then for London. Dear Virginia, I am always happy with Peter, with our three magnificent children and I give thanks to the whole Heaven. I wish so much a new child, but it is not coming! How do you explain it? What a pity! Pray for me that the Lord may grant this grace to me."

Her children are respectively, four and a half, three and a half and two months of age. In the summer, Gianna goes with them to Cormayeur. One night, after putting them to bed, she wrote to Peter: "How beautiful to be able to stay with the children everyday and night and care for them and enjoy them. I understand how much it displeases you when, returning home at night, you cannot enjoy them at least for a while. They are so happy to have their mother near them and all for themselves. They are really three treasures. Unfortunately you, my fourth treasure, my beloved Pedrin, are missing! My thoughts are with you often and I am near you with my heart and prayer. Do not get too tired!"

Some days afterwards, from July 11–18, Gianna accompanied Peter on a journey to Denmark and Sweden. This time also, the children are entrusted in good hands, to the friend Mariuccia Parmeggiani and in the company of her children. However, she returns soon to see them and she enjoys being with them.

## FOURTH MATERNITY

After a few days, Gianna realizes she is pregnant. She experiences an immense joy. Finally her prayer was granted. She feels very well, and goes for long walks with her children and friends. The pregnancy seems not to give her any problem. One day, however, she had the impression of a strange swelling on the abdomen which did not seem natural. She reveals it to her husband thinking it could be an ovarian cyst. At once, it was decided to have a check-up at Magenta. Gianna left again once more her children to Savina and Mariuccia. Who better than them can take care of the children?

Her brother, Dr. Ferdinand, accompanied and assists her. At once, he realizes that near the uterus a great fibroma was growing producing very painful colic. He had Professor Vitali, a gynecologist, examine her. Unfortunately, he confirms the previous prognosis and advises immediate surgery. Gianna, who is a doctor herself, was aware of the gravity of her case. Professor Vitali clearly tells her what is going to happen to her and her child in her womb if pregnancy continues. A pitiless truth which makes all despondent. Gianna is strongly shaken.

But after the first bewilderment, the light of faith shines, she puts faith in Providence which can do everything, can cure even with a miraculous sign. Gianna, then hopes, but God's will be always done! Her convictions are well rooted. How many mothers she had comforted and exhorted with her medical skill and her advice! Now is her turn to witness her love for life, to affirm the right to life to the unborn child.

With her husband and her brother Dr. Ferdinand, she tells Professor Vitali that the life of the child should prevail over hers. It is a sin to kill in the womb. These were her sacred convictions. She was always pro-life, respecting the Law of God: "Do not kill."

It had happened once in the clinic that a young lady came complaining of abdominal pains. Gianna understood that a procured miscarriage was on the way. Becoming sad, she exclaimed to the young lady: "Don't you regret having offended God? Why have you done this? It was your creature! Are you really repentant? Have you begged pardon to God? Did you confess this sin?"

As they began the necessary surgery on Gianna, they found a great uterine fibroma. With skill, the surgeon cut off the great neoplastic mass, making a perfect hemostasis without injuring the uterine cavity. He sutured with great care the edges of the wound in order to allow the continuation of pregnancy. Some people, fearing for Gianna's life, prayed for a natural abortion.

They were tremendous days of passion, but borne with faith. "Dear Mariuccia," she writes to her friend to whom she had entrusted her children in the mountains, "You can guess what I experience in these days; how my heart and thought are always turned to my dearest three treasures. I trust in the Lord and the Blessed Mother of Guerison. Ask my "puppies" to pray. Many great kisses from mamma."

Eight days after the operation, she writes: "Infinite thanks for what you are doing for my treasures, whom I am certain have found in you a second mother. The professor has not yet told me when he would let me go. As for the surgery, all went well...but to take a trip up to the Courmayeur, even using all my good will, I really doubt I should do it. It could be imprudent." She also sent a letter to Mariuccia with some thoughts for her children: "Dear treasures of mine, father will bring you my great kisses; I would like so much to go there myself, but I have to stay in bed because I still have some inconveniences. Be good, be obedient to Mariuccia and to Savina. Pierluigi who is the eldest, should make the little sisters play without quarreling.

"Mariolina who is the next in age should be obliging to Lauretta. I have you in my heart and I think of you at every moment. Say a Hail Mary, your mother."

From her bed of suffering, Gianna prays. To busy herself, not being able to sleep, she writes as she can. She writes to Fr. Albert that she is getting better and that she entrusts herself to the Virgin Mary. To Zita, she repeats that if the newborn is a boy, she will name him Henry and she hopes and prays that he may become a priest. She reveals to some of the many persons who visit her ardent desire to have a son priest, "I have suffered much, but I am happy because maternity is saved. I wish a boy to be born and I would like him to be a priest, Henry, the baptismal name of my brother who is a missionary."

Apparently cured, Gianna returns to her treasures at home. Gradually, she seemed to recover her health and resumed her habitual occupations: in the clinic, visiting people, caring with more love for her own family. From time to time, with her car, she takes her children to Zita, the patient and affectionate Auntie Zita. In the ancestral home there is a large garden where the children can run and gather flowers to give to mother when she comes to join them.

The last months of Gianna's life remained memorable especially in the mind and heart of Mariuccia Parmeggiani, with whom she had frequent encounters, and with Savina Passeri, the maid she loved as if she had been her sister. She recalls to mind: "In the morning, she would stay home with her children and me. In the afternoon, she would daily go to the clinic. My Lady was a very good person. She was always happy. In spite of the confidence which in time resulted between us two, she never made me understand the drama she was living. When at home, she would always help me... My Mistress had always been a mother to me. How much good she also did to my brothers, to my parents. How great was her help to us. I will always be grateful to her, even though now she is no longer with us.

Mariuccia Parmeggiana exclaims with a sigh: "We were so close to each other! Today, there are no longer friendships so beautiful! "

## THE GIFT OF LIFE

On Holy Friday she is on the Cross with Jesus. On April 20, 1961, Holy Friday, Gianna enters the Hospital of Monza to undergo an unavoidable surgery which could not be delayed. She reveals all her courage and her faith in God.

Before entering the hospital, she prayed much and made people pray for her, desirous to be a mother for the fourth time. Her expectation is great and joyful because the children are gifts of God to her. She has entrusted her first three children, her joy, her crown, to the care of her sister Zita. Life which blooms and grows is her declared passion. The months of the fourth gestation were lived with her heart in her throat, but with bright faith. An ugly illness, a voluminous fibroid at the uterus, threatens her life and the one of her unborn baby, in her womb.

To the eyes of the unbeliever, a fibrous tumor is a tragedy, against which people curse with anger. Gianna, instead, does not curse, and her own family does the same, and they pray and hope. "How much you have suffered without a complaint! How many prayers were said that the child be born healthy and normal and his or her life be saved. It was your full trust in the Lord that gave you strength and control of yourself in this long and painful expectation. You loved your dear children no less than the creature you bore in your bosom. For months and months you prayed the Lord, the Virgin Mary and your mother so that the guarantee and the right to life of the little unborn child be preserved without claiming the sacrifice of your life and spared you for our children and our family."

On Holy Friday, the day in which we celebrate the supreme Divine Sacrifice, Gianna is aware she is going to face her holocaust. "Sister," she at once says to the nurse-sister who comes to accompany her to the obstetrics department, "Sister, I have come here, this time, to die."

To this serious eventuality she prepared herself spiritually and materially, surrendering, as usual, to the will of God. Though it is true that the spirit is willing, the flesh, however, is weak.

Engineer Molla, in his memoirs describes those months preceding the climbing of Gianna to her Calvary: "With incomparable determination of soul and with unshakable determination, you have continued your motherly and professional mission, to the last days of gestation.

"You were praying and meditating. I remember that habitual smile of yours, and your customary serenity for beauty, the health and vivacity of our children were sometimes clouded with a continuous worry. You feared and were anxious that your little child could be born unhealthy.

You were praying and praying that this should not happen.

"Several times you begged me pardon for causing worries to me. You told me that never like then, you needed gentleness and understanding. You never uttered a word on your part to me, in those long months of your awareness, as a doctor, of what was in store for you. I'm sure you did this not to make me suffer more. I was worried for that silent putting everything in order at home, day after day, every corner of our home, every drawer, every personal object, as if you were undertaking a long trip. But I did not dare ask anything nor the reason for it."

An almost identical witnessing is provided by Savina Passeri, the faithful servant: "I recall to mind that she placed all she had in precise order. She fixed the drawers of the cabinet even if it was not needed. I questioned myself how all this should have come to her mind. Only when she died, it came to my mind that she felt that, after the birth of the child she was expecting, she would never come back home..."

Gianna then leaves all in order: Peter's

coats and trousers, the dresses of her children. It seems she wishes to see again and again things prepared with so much love, with such precision, as if she was about to initiate a long trip, with no chance of coming back. A definitive departure.

## SAVE THE CHILD!

"Before going to the hospital," Savina remembers, she told me: "I recommend the children..." She was at peace, or thus it seemed. She worked so much till the last day. Thus she prepared herself, without neglecting her duty as a doctor, spouse and mother, exercised with so much love."

"Either I or him," like a hammering temptation never left her. Gianna, the strong woman, though always trusting in Providence, has decided it long in the past, because she believes in the miracle of the growing life. To her sister Virginia, she says: "Keep in mind if they would ask you which of the two should be saved, do not hesitate, "the child first!" And to the husband before the delivery, with a firm and serene tone, with a profound look which he will never forget, "If you have to decide between the child and me, no mistake, I expect from you to decide for the life of the child. Save him!"

This solemn determination cannot be explained without a great faith, without a Christian hope based on the resurrection of Christ, without a great love for God and his creatures.

Aware of the impending danger, to a friend who had advised her to save herself, she answers with determination: "No, No! I want the child to live!"

In the afternoon of that Holy Friday, Professor Mario Vitali decides to have the delivery in a natural form. But the hours passed by between hopes and delusions till the next day April 21. At 11:00, after the caesarian cut, comes to the light a beautiful child, a girl. She weighs four kilograms and a half. She will be called by the will of her father, Gianna-Emmanuela: Gianna in remembrance of the mother and Emmanuela to remember the presence of Christ among us, also in the most difficult moments of life.

That Holy Saturday, prelude of Easter, sees life bloom from the long sacrifice of a mother. Jesus speaking of his death, explained, "If the grain of wheat fallen to the ground does not die, it remains alone; if it dies, it yields much fruit."

Gianna loves life, but she loves more to do the will of God. It is a familiar refrain in her lips: "What God wishes!" Her sister Zita reminds us: "Gianna used to repeat: What God wishes! Jesus in the Garden of Gethsemane had prayed the Father to take away the bitter chalice of His passion and death, and He was heard because of His reverence." (Hb. 5, 7), that is, He was delivered from the power of death having His Father change his sacrifice into a glorious exaltation. So Gianna, extending her week of passion which began the day she was operated on seven months before to a few days after Easter, prays with a heavy heart that the chalice be taken away, not so much to flee from personal suffering, but for the suffering of her Peter and of her children still so young. She generated her children in suffering (all her pregnancies had been a risk), and the deliveries had been very difficult. She too, like Jesus, was granted that from her holocaust many mothers could draw the strength and courage to affirm the right of innocent creatures to life. The worthy husband will write: "The Lord heard you, but this divine grace claimed the offering of your life. And you have done it."

Professor Mario Vitali, with great admiration and honesty, in the presence of Gianna, Francis and Ferdinand, with great sincerity and honesty, exclaims, "Behold the Catholic Mother!" And the nurses commented: "It is the first time we see a person enter the operating room so calmly..." The chaplain, Fr. M. Cazzaniga testifies, "for several days the attitude of Gianna, (who as a doctor was well aware of her grave condition), was of serenity and of joy for the decision she had taken.

"Among all women, the one who left in me the best and unforgettable remembrance is Dr. Gianna Beretta. As soon as she arrived at the hospital, she manifested her will to offer her life for the normal birth and the life of her child."

After the difficult delivery and the effect of the narcotics, she felt severe pains in her abdomen caused by the septic peritonitis. The first biographers and the prudent testimonies of family members and intimate friends who had assisted her, underline the circumstance of the Pascal hallelujah of the Risen Lord with Gianna's hallelujah of joy and suffering. She had the little baby in her arms and kept looking at her a long time with untold tenderness and love. She caressed her lightly, without saying a word. Other people will take care of her, not she, but faith tells her she will see her from Heaven and take care of her for ever.

## THE LONG AGONY

Her long agony begins soon after. Her sister Zita affirms that Gianna "due to very severe pains, and above all for the thought to have to leave her children, invoked her mother. Perhaps she had asked her for the power to resist so great a pain." Also sister Virginia arrives from India, unaware of the family's tragedy. On Easter Tuesday, as soon as she enters the room of her suffering sister, she is welcomed with these words: "Finally you are here! If you knew, Gina, how much one suffers to have to die when one has to leave behind children so young!"

The great suffering returns, but she is also comforted by the thought of God who will not abandon her children: there is Zita.

Her sister will take care of the children. This is her testament: "I entrust to you my little angels. Place Gigi to sleep in my bed, in the room near by, with the three girls." To sister Virginia, doctor and the Canossian sister, she says confidentially: "Do not go away any longer. Tell your Provincial to give you work in Milan, so you too will help to educate my children. "

Gianna accepts to live consciously the drama of her last hours of life. Like Jesus. "I can't stand it any longer, I am no longer capable to react." She surrenders to suffering. However, she refuses to be treated with narcotics. She wishes to drink the bitter chalice to the dregs, if this is the will of God. Her brother Doctor Ferdinand confirms:

"During the atrocious abdominal sufferings caused by the skeptic peritonitis, Gianna begged the doctors attending her not to put her under the action of the narcotics, because they would not allow her to be conscious all the way to death. Not only she never refused to submit herself to the attempts to keep her alive, nor she ever complained, with great admiration of all those who treated her medically.

"Everything possible was attempted to save her. Never a complaint. When some words or small complaint is about to betray her she puts a handkerchief in her mouth. She wishes to drink the bitter chalice of suffering like Jesus, though within human limitations, as if completing in her body what was missing to the passion of Christ."

## AN UNBROKEN DIALOGUE WITH GOD

On the morning of April 25, after a sleepless tormented night, Gianna recovers a little. She sees Peter near her and with gentle serenity, which seem beyond earth, she confides to her husband: "Peter, now I am cured. Peter I was in the hereafter and if you knew what I have seen! One day I'll tell you. But as we were too happy, we were too complacent with our marvelous children, full of health and grace, filled with all the heavenly blessings, they have sent me back down here to suffer a little more, because it is not right to present oneself to the Lord without much suffering."

Peter, one day will declare: "How much

it meant to me her testament of joy and of suffering." He kept continuously near her: "From that moment, I am sure, Gianna never ceased her dialogue with the Lord and her communication with Heaven, in her suffering and agony. She no longer wished to be caressed and kissed by me: she was already belonging to Heaven."

The love of Gianna for Peter and Peter for Gianna and of both for their family has its deep roots in the love of God, according to St. Augustine's thought, "We love one another because we love God, if we do not love God first, Who is Love, how can we truly love?"

Their lives give testimony, first they have loved God who is the source of love. In life as well as in death Gianna had God as the first, absolute, undisputed love. From this love, springs forth love for her dear ones, for her spouse, for her children, for the neighbor, for the poor, the sick, and the weak.

Now, this is sublimated love, on her death bed as if it were a calvary, with the full acceptance of God's will. She seems to think on God who was for her infinitely rich of graces, having her to be born in an exceptional family, and above all making her meet Peter and giving her the joy of being a mother.

Her sister Virginia was always at her bedside, with a beautiful crucifix to have her kiss it. Virginia with a soft voice suggested her thought of faith, exhorts her to beg pardon of every small fault. Gianna pressed that crucifix in her hands, kisses it again and again with ineffable transport. It seems that in so doing she is alleviated, "If you knew, Gina, what a consolation I feel kissing the Crucifix! O, if there were no Jesus who consoles us at these moments!"

Of the Crucifix, she certainly is an Icon on that new Calvary. She could repeat with St. Paul: "I was crucified with Christ and it is no longer I who live, but Christ lives in me. I live this life of the flesh in the faith of the Son of God. He has loved me and has given Himself for me."

But perhaps she did not even think of it. What is certain is that she wished to do the will of God, and she did it. Now, it seems that everything becomes relative for her before God. Always to her sister Virginia, she confides: "If you knew how one judges things differently on the death bed. How vain seems certain things to which we give much importance in the world!"

## LORD, MY LORD! MOTHER!

She repeatedly asks for Holy Communion. She had received It with faith and love everyday; now however she cannot receive It because of the continuous vomiting. It seems that God is hiding from her in the supreme moment of life. She asks that if she cannot swallow that Bread of Life, at least she asks to place It on her thirsty tongue, just to touch Him. She is satisfied in her wish. Not only on that moment so solemn, filled with the presence of God, but also after the Host is no longer present, Peter will hear his Gianna mumble: "Jesus, I love you! I love you!"

But the trials are not yet finished for this ardent soul with love and faith. There is still the painful doubt that her holocaust be badly interpreted as an injustice towards her children whom she is about to abandon and towards her husband. This time too we listen to the testimony written by her very same husband, Peter. It is a spiritual dialogue uttered shortly before death, with his dearly beloved, already turned to Heaven:

"You were offering the holocaust of your life. And you were offering this holocaust with the deep pain of a spouse who has to leave her children and the family and the most dear things given you by God. You were offering it asking from your fullness of trust in Providence, from your humility, from prayer, from faith that the doubt that your sacrifice was an act of injustice toward the children whom you were leaving orphan, and towards our family and toward me, would be taken away.

Peter knows and testifies that the act of Gianna's heroic charity to save the creature to be born was in harmony with the will of God and not an act of injustice toward the children and towards him who was sharing in the same faith.

"You were considering your motherly duty to care, to educate, and to form our children not less serious than the duty to guarantee their coming to life after conception. You knew well that the motherly contribution in caring, educating, and forming our children could not be substituted. But in your humility and, above all in the plenitude of your trust in Providence, you have acquired the conviction not to commit any act of injustice and of lack of charity towards our children because Providence would never fail to substitute your visible presence.

"You were aware of not committing any act of injustice towards me, because you rightly considered me in the duty of accepting the will of God no less than you, and because you knew that I, though in great pain, was taking into account your faith and that I was not opposing the heroism of your charity."

The nurse in charge of the gynecological department summarized the sunset of this heroic mother in these words:

"She never complained of anything. She was aware of everything, when the effect of the anesthesia would come to an end she would remain quiet, aware, silent, in an attitude of listening, of prayer..

"When we used the thermometer or listened to her pulse, and did any other service, she would let us do it, but with her look would make us understand that it was all of no avail.'

The moment came that she could no longer speak. Sister Virginia comforted her: "Take courage Gianna! Father and mother are in Heaven and they are waiting for you. Are you happy to go there?" From the movement of the eyelashes we could read her full adhesion to the will of God. All life long she said "yes" to God in the varied circumstances of her life. That final yes, loaded with love, is the shining and radiant ray which makes us foresee a splendid morning in the joy of paradise.

On the morning of April 28, Gianna was brought home in an ambulance. She was agonizing. She was brought home, having repeatedly expressed the desire to close her eyes where she had lived as a spouse and as a happy mother. She was aware of everything. Perhaps she hoped to hear her children call "mother!"

They woke up before the usual time, at dawn, perhaps at the unusual bustling of people coming and going. Perhaps they had the intuition of that loved presence who is about to leave them definitively. The decision was made to take her away to other relatives. They did not have the courage to let the children see their dying mother, who in turn understood their decision. The noise of the car engine is heard then faded away.

Now she can say with Jesus: "Consummatum est." It is all finished. Father in your hands I commend my spirit."

An hour later, at about 8, she closed her eyes to this world darkened at her demise, to reopen in the glaring light of Heaven. She was 38 years six months of age.

## GIANNA CONTINUES TO SPEAK

Jesus, speaking of His death on the cross, a sacrifice offered to the Father for the life of the world, said: "When I am lifted up from the earth, I will draw everybody to me."

Thinking on the holocaust of Gianna, chosen disciple of Jesus, we cannot but meditate again those words of the Lord. Embracing the will of God, Gianna has taken the Cross and has followed the Master up to Golgotha. Tragically expired on that Saturday, now she is placed in a room where the candles are burning. Her face was astonishingly serene, every sign of pain was gone. She seemed full of joy as when she was in the mountains, near her treasures, the children. Stretched down on the rocks or on the grass, she would close her eyes while the bright rays of the sun would cover her face.

Near, there is another room, a bigger one, the children's toy room where she played with them and their little friends so often and with an inexhaustible love.

An interminable line of people, in tears and praying begins to march, a procession of piety and prayer. The procession becomes more numerous the following day, and continues unbroken until Monday, April 30, the funeral day.

## TWO PROCESSION

In those sad hours, the rays of faith give bright light to the Beretta's and the Molla's families. In the afternoon of that Sunday, humanly gray, but sparkling with Christian light, the long procession of people who want to see Gianna and pray and give her thanks, grows more and more. Another reduced procession is on the way: Peter and the relatives come to bring the newly born child. They go in haste toward the small church of the Virgin Mary of Good Council. They are bringing the newly born girl to the baptismal fount, where God's children Pierluigi, Mariolina, and Lauretta were regenerated.

Now the new child is in the arms of Aunt Zita. Pierluigi holds the basin on his small knees, that basin which Gianna, on other occasions, had prepared with so much love. All are present: Peter, the children, the aunts and uncles. It is the same Fr. Giuseppe that, as he did with the first three children, now administers the Sacrament of Baptism which makes us children of God.

To the fourth child is given the name of Gianna Emmanuela: the first name, in remembrance of the mother and her sacrifice; the second, to reaffirm their faith in the presence of God in the family and in the hearts of the members of the family. Peter, holds the candle, symbol of faith, not shaken by the sad events, but reinforced in trial.

Immediately afterwards, as it was done for the other children, Peter, head of the family, and because he was asked by Gianna, pronounces before the image of the Virgin Mary of Good Council the Act of Consecration. Thus, the child has two mothers in Heaven who watch over her.

In the face of so vivid a faith, one remains wondering and praising God who never abandons his children in trials, but encourages and consoles them making clearer to their eyes the reality of a joyous hope.

The small procession goes back home. No exterior celebration. The spirit of Gianna, spouse and mother is felt, motherly hovering over her family

Pierluigi, contemplating his mother in the coffin, turned to his father to exclaim: "Why, is mother there? Is she mother? Does mother see me, touch me, think of me?" Peter has a naught in his throat and is not able to answer. Dear creature Pierluigi, when he says in his innocence, "For mother there should be a golden little house!"

## A TRIUMPH OF FAITH AND PRAYER

As in the preceding narration, we let the witnesses speak, relatives and friends and those who had great esteem for

Gianna. First of all her husband Peter. His testimony of those days was very concise: "On Saturday, Sunday, and Monday, there was all an endless procession of people, men and women, old and young and children, prayerful, crying and invoking. The parish priest of Ponte Nuovo declared to have never had so many Easter confessions as this year. Many men confided that they felt the need to go to confession before paying the last visit to her. Her funeral has been a triumph of faith and prayers, of emotions and example."

Ada Deitinger, who knew and esteemed Gianna left this testimony: "I saw her again dead: she was beautiful, very beautiful with her face thinned by her illness, she was still preserving and diffusing her peaceful smile. Her funeral had been a triumph, and I, though my heart was pierced by grief, rejoiced to collect the testimonies of so many workers, men and women, all addressed to exalt her humble goodness."

They testified that: "She did not expect to be served. When we would go to her house to repair something out of order, she would clean where we had left some dirt. A woman like this should not have died.

She had only one fault, to be too good."

Doctor Golanda Botti, a pediatric who was present at the funerals, declared: "Monday was an unforgettable day, in the splendor of the afternoon, that long prayerful procession, in a painful recollection behind her who was passing for the last time among the persons who loved her, almost to give them the last blessing. I believe that the remembrance of Gianna will be the seed of much good. We cannot think that God has taken away so noble and loved a creature without a high motive that, for the time being, is hidden to us."

A friend and collaborator in Catholic Action, Enrica Parmigiani, writes: "I have seen her in the sleep of the saints, with her face still irradiated by an angelic smile, surrounded by flowers with no sign of death."

In this world, a superficial world, Gianna's sacrifice made a great impression. Yes, on that day it was spoken not so much of death, but of sacrifice. On a board written in big letters, hanging on the facade of the church of Our Lady of Good Council, where Gianna so many times had indulged in prayer, it was written: "Profoundly touched, we remember Doctor

Gianna Molla Beretta, who with full awareness offered herself for the life of her daughter Gianna Emmanuela."

The workers of the SAFFA factory consider her a martyr. Everybody knew her. They knew of her goodness, her dispensability towards the poor, the children, and those in need, in general. The vice president of the SAFFA, Mario Varisco, speaking a few days afterward at the Rotary Club of Magenta, interprets their sentiments with these words: "If the event of death usually causes compassion, this, which touches us closely, is much more moving when we think on the act done by a mother who, fully aware of the risk she was going to face, has sacrificed herself to give life to a new creature. People from every walk of life who surrounded the large building of the factory were aware of this sacrifice. I have seen a political party being suspended. Just on that day in which the lamented doctor took her place among the angels of paradise and was irradiating the light of a star on earth; consoler of the tears of a father resigned to live in endless sorrow. The political rally changed into a sorrowful procession to the funeral parlor where lay the body of that noble lady who all through her life shared the treasures of her goodness with the many who would come to her for their physical health and for their children."

The funeral ceremony was a choir glorifying in sad notes the memory which expresses human grief, as it was the weeping of Christ at the tomb of Lazarus, but at the same time it confessed the exaltation of the believers' faith.

The small church is absolutely incapable of holding the crowd of those who by prayer wanted to greet the martyr mother, the one who to their judgment had been and angel of goodness and of generosity.

Surrounding Peter were Pierluigi, Mariolina, the brothers and sisters Beretta and many relatives and friends. The priest who was presiding had not the heart to say a few words. The more eloquent sermon is the one of the crowd, devout and meditative. It did not look a sad rite, but a solemn Pascal liturgy, because everybody was convinced that Heaven was enriched with a new saint.

Sister Virginia, writing to her brother Fr.

Albert informs him that the funeral had been more beautiful than one for a princess and an incentive to a strong return to God, to sacramental life. There were never so many Easter confessions as in those days! These men confided to the sacristan that they felt the need to go to Confession before they dared look at the corpse of Gianna. It is the same testimony Peter made to his children. Those workers and groups of people will later have Holy Masses celebrated, as a pledge of gratitude to her.

The coffin, covered with red roses, symbol of her husband's love was placed over the tomb of the priests, under the altar. This was an unusual decision, not only because the Molla family did not have a chapel, but especially for the esteem and veneration of everybody, including the clergy, convinced that those mortal remains were relics of a holy martyr.

This was the conviction above all of those persons who knew her. Again, her sister Virginia, writing to Fr. Albert, expresses her own opinion: "Our Gianna honors us and there is nothing left than rejoicing for the great glory she was able to give to God with her holy life and heroic death. From Heaven her function of mother did not end, it has only changed the way and field to exercise it. Dear Gianna, help us all to reach heaven..."

Zita, the sister to whom Gianna had entrusted the care and education of her children, is certain that the Lord wants to make of her an example of mother to be imitated. "If the Lord called her with Him, it is because He wants to make her an example to many mothers who find themselves in such predicaments."

## HEAVEN REJOICES

Fr. Albert, too, from the Brazilian Missions, after receiving the news of the demise of his sister gives way to his human and Christian sentiments:

"We cry but the whole paradise rejoices, on witnessing her arriving there, close to God, a luminous star. Tonight more than celebrating Holy Mass for her seventh day, I would like to celebrate the Mass for the Holy Angels. You will see, Peter, how she will help you more in everything and how she will assist your children. Notwithstanding that we all feel she is in Heaven, let us continue to pray and make people pray.

I think on the grief of Pierluigi, who being so intelligent, might have understood much more than his small sisters, tell him that I remember him always and that mother is always near him, though he does not see her, likewise his guardian angel."

The same thoughts are expressed by the other brother Fr. Joseph to his brother-in-law. "Dear Peter, you have a saint in Heaven who will do nothing else but pray for you and for your little angels. Have faith and be always serene..."

To end, we report a last testimony of parents and friends given with the conviction of the sanctity of this exceptional mother. The Guzzetti family of Ponte Nuovo, the same day of Gianna's holy death writes to Engineer Peter: "Allow us to manifest what our hearts have experienced. We feel it a duty to do so, though the social condition is very great, we think God wanted her with Him. You have lost not a wife as all have, but an angel. Be comforted by the remembrance of her generous heart, her spiritual riches and her sacred maternity. Accept her sublime and supreme sacrifice. It is mainly the preciosity of her life which gives value to her great sacrifice. Let us invoke from God and from Gianna resignation from God and from your dear One, who is no  longer on earth but in Paradise. She has given everything to the Lord. The Lord accepted her holocaust so that many sinners may be converted. She has left behind her a path of virtue. We believe she was a chosen soul and we will invoke her in difficult moments as a saint."

## GLORIFICATION IN THE YEAR DEDICATED TO THE FAMILY

During the year 1993 and in the early months of 1994, articles celebrating venerable Gianna Beretta Molla multiplied. A diffuse sense not only of admiration but also of Christian hope touched this society so neglectful of true values.

Winter is passing away and after unending falls of rain the flowers are blooming. On April 24, 1994 a "sign of the times" appeared in St. Peter's Square.

It was a magnificent day, it was a celebration of faith among people of every race and culture. Innumerable people came to assist at the beatification of three witnesses of faith: A catechist martyr from Zaire; a mother, Elisabetta Canori Mora, from Rome, and our Gianna.

Gianna is one of most beautiful fruits relatives

were part of the offertory procession.

At the closing of the solemn ceremony of beatification, the Pope welcomed the husband and children of Gianna Beretta Molla with other members of the family.

The Pope, at the end of his homily, said: "She had the grace of a united family, rich in faith and love. She was a happy mother, but a trial was waiting for her in the fourth pregnancy. In the dramatic choice between saving her life and that of the creature she had in her womb, she did not hesitate to immolate herself. What a heroic witnessing is hers, a true hymn to life, in contrast with a certain mentality rampant today. May her sacrifice infuse courage in those who devote themselves, with personal and unselfish commitment, to the Pro-Life Movement and other similar organizations so that the intangibility of the dignity of every human existence be recognized from the moment of conception to natural death as a priority value, as a basis for the respect due to any other human and social right."